First published in 2024 by

Schism prεss²

First edition
ISBN: 9798880408122

Cover design by GJS
Cover images and frontispiece by RC Miller

Printed in London, UK.

Thickening

RC Miller

SCHISM^2

no desire to die
no desire to live
the wind blows over me

— Taneda Santōka

CONTENTS

Life in a Pond

Chewed Eyeball Clot

Automatic Hallways

Life in a Pond

YEARS TO GO

The usual weather makes me shit and fish
Sorrow, crustaceans, secretions and extinctions.

The usual platters make fish shit
Paper bags full of human hair.

The usual splatter tells me not to get too heavy.
There's freedom in being killed by what killed you
before.

THE PLAGUE

There's sanitizer in your car.
I give you a hard time about it,
But I'm loving your rough hands.

A dead pigeon
Is talking to you and sleeping against you
As the bag it's in is tossed out the car door.

A dragonfly
Gets cremated.
Lamps and rocks lay eggs in the binge.

An all new wind
Blows random pain.

NO DELAY LUNCH BUFFET

Turns the house of God into a place of violence.
Don't worry about dying, you weren't meant to live anyway.

FISHING BLUES

Henry Thomas didn't swallow
And he was gone before tomorrow.
My laptop is breaking my heart.
I'm gonna marry it before I'm replaced.

Then our love will ride some side of the road
Raccoon carcass anxious to butter coils.
But love loses all meaning when two carts of Prime groceries
Are being carted across a Whole Foods parking lot.

There's this little girl watching her phone in one shopping cart,
But she can't talk on her phone because her language has changed.
She's one of lots of little girls needed to buy phones
When there's lots of packaging needed to make meals at home.

Henry Thomas broke my heart.
And I can't sleep no more, laptop sweetheart.
There's lots of unborn little girls needing to buy phones and die at home.
Any fish bite if you got good bait.

PISS JAR

Time passes.
I can't grasp it.
The past grows.
I'm asking for mercy.

The present passes
A past asking for mercy.
I'm not somewhere else
Ever since I've been a part of it.

GOODBYE AND HELLO

A duck quacks
On the river bank
And digs out a snail from its shell.
The duck sucks the snail from its shell,
Quacks and shits and fucks the river bank.

The river sucks the snail's shell from its shore.
The sucked shell brings its lips to the river's mortal
  soul.
The river is celebrating today as the day
The snail chose to ignore.
I'm letting go of me somehow.

LIVING

I see a frozen duck dinner in my mirror.
It's stinging, I'm singing.
No way to ever know any duck at the mirror.
No way to really know when you're frozen or a dinner
  so I'm winning.

Flies in the shopping center deposit chicken sandwich
  diapers.
I pity fully born things having various stores to settle
  in.
A rock by a stagnant pond counting on its natural
  smashing
Is the unreadable living of my head.

MEMBERSHIP RENEWAL BILL

My neighbor's refurbished kitchen floor
Has a carpet of patterns
Of all the seagull intestines I've seen before.

Intestines instead of dawn
Caramelize and I love
Spring rains whisking me to kitchen floors I've fucked on before.

Intestines come out wrong
As I laugh when I think about
How seagulls will hack at my dead body.

All the lovers I used to be with have it easier.

EELS

Add cow hair
To a doll's head the size of a moldy hand.
Abyss mutilations wad commercials where
Tingling TV's wildly tickle
Chewed eyeballs in lingerie
From an old country waltz.
There's more places I'd like to see.
There's more places I'd like to be.
There's more places behind me.

FROM A LONG, WEARY DREAM

I beat off in a rented room for two years alone.
I think of my life and my failure to make new life.
My phone offers some love between my legs.
She sure does seem to miss me at home.

I cut off my legs to imagine
I see something better in everyone.
But I'm wrong to see anything in anyone
Except the dog ahead in the dog's behind.

I beat off in a bed and pleasure my phone.
I imagine an owl with a black fingernail
Finger-fucking a black owl.
Kiss your husband goodbye.

I'LL NEVER SEE PEOPLE ANYMORE

I eat a vegetable, then love my grim existence.
A cat roars as I stuff it with fruits
That can't stop talking about themselves.
Some wall of an airplane on fire
Disappears into its predictable plot.
Foot odors once prevalent there
Now live spine free.
That's the best you can do when you leave
Everyone that's ever loved you.

I DON'T WORRY ABOUT BEAUTY ANYMORE

I open my mouth and death jumps in.
I'm open to death
That walks a frog and then watches YouTube.

Bloodworms and phantoms
Suck insect larvae.
Invertebrates bloom as daylight

On the concrete that filled the pond
Suspends larvae
Blooming inside two people growing apart.

WALNUT GRAVE YOGURT

Covers flat frog petroglyphs
Drying once they realize their ratings.
Nights become me stealing
My girlfriend's tail and fashioning a canoe from it.
Then my girlfriend's tail quiets down.
Then there's this obscene dance we do that listens in
On flat frogs crawling over flat lawns.
Yeah, there are better things to dance to
But the planet's dead.

MORNING OF DEPARTURE

A man wandering the PATH in Manhattan was sliced in half by an oncoming train early Tuesday while some other riders watched and went.

The victim, who had walked the tracks from 23rd Street, was attempting to howl.

A source said the body's separate halves were left lying opposite one another in the northbound and southbound tracks.

It was clear what the halves were doing to each other.

It was clear that the other riders have never been sliced in half.

And you and I, we've never truly loved anyone.

A PARKING LOT IS PARKING PEOPLE

2-inch long insects are fond of being pan-fried and
skewered for an on-the-go treat.

Parked people compare them to a popcorn-y flavor
without the butter.

Insects fill their lives up with things they can feel but
just cannot touch.

Some orange-and-black ones are locked in a deadly
embrace with a mouse on the road in a diseased
country.

People park, drop by drop, to watch the struggle, torn
further apart by the fiery wheels inside them.

Death and decay.

Insects compare it to a popcorn-y flavor with the
butter.

Staying all day if they want to.

HOLIDAYS

From a hospital bed on Christmas Day via a crooked video,
My grandfather wishes me a happy birthday.
My uncle reminds him it's not my birthday but Christmas
So my grandfather says who's Ryan, ah shit,
Turn your fucking iPhone off.

Then it's New Year's Eve and my girlfriend has morning sickness,
But I say it's the sickness of a rotten furnace
Sabotaging our air with the boiling bones below us.
What could we want with all these bones before us?
Let's stand in line until we can't care for ourselves anyway.

Every time I turn my fucking iPhone on
My grandfather sings to me for the final time after
I filmed his timeless lines.
Will you tell me where all the people have gone?
Did I hear my little baby cry?

IMMORTALITY

I saw on the internet that I still care.
On the internet, there's so many wounds to recover
  from.
I saw a billion frozen pizzas that look like me.
It's a shame that one-billion frozen pizzas die easier
  than me.

I saw from my drunken texts to you that I don't wanna
  eat tonight
Cause eating is about being found out.
I said Russell Edson has pointy Asian nipples like
  yours and
I wish I could tell you what his nipples are there for.

A frozen pizza is eating the idea of itself.
Pointy Asian nipples are easy to find online.
The internet goes on and on as I try to recover from
My birth.

LIFE IS PRECIOUS

My freezer saved
Chiggers in an icecap sag.
This apartment complex bush
Fell asleep but didn't get eaten by worms.

My freezer is layered with
Nazi literature in America.
Nazi's stay around in town
To fake one instacart grocery trip after another.

I sniff my woman's pussy because she begs me to.
I bite my woman's clit because I love to.
Pussy juices in our apartment remind me life ends too
fast.
I woke up this morning to find out I was only a dream.

POND FOOD

I pull down my pants and piss grief.
My throat is sliced open
By the piss flowing down her legs.
Our hearts cry as a sliced-winged sun
Shines and shapes its wet ass.
A coffin full of shit
Gets hard and pays for
Green eyes eating living flesh.
Coffins don't know any better.
They're the kind of love that quickly moves on.

HURRYING AWAY FROM THE EARTH

An opened belly snacks on saliva.
Your ass is my goddess.
Lick my balls slowly
In the soft water.
I drink from your slit throat.
Multiple cocks sprout
From your naked thighs.

An anus with empty voices
Loses its bones to the wind.
I want nothing to do with this world.
My heart is cold and inhuman.
The sky's fat ass
Smells like the bird's death
Lining my blindfold.

SOLITUDE

An inbred row of shadows
Eating a set of perched dentures
On the summit of a straw cock
Is one of my small sufferings tonight.

SLEEPLESS NIGHT

My lover without lips
Is a little bird ripping out its own eyes.
Constant feelings of terror
Is what my life insists.
Purplish donkeys
Sneezing skin.
Bloody skinned mud
Lowered by
A skull's dripping nose.
My lover's asshole is the toilet
For my trail of sperm,
Between moons
With no direction home.

I DO NOT DIE I AM NOTHING

I put on my dress
In the body of a bird.
My thumbs in thorns,
My ass in a mouth.
I shave your tits
With my balls at dawn.

The universe is limp.
I am blacker than never-ending thorns.
I put on my body
A quesadilla in the forest
Sung about by blind gray alligators
Evolving from bee cleavages.

POEM FOR INSANE TIMES

Sunfish and dragons make disgusting music
Aborted babies learn.
Angels on a tapestry

With seared bones.
Their long icy blood
Like a viper free in the wind

Hungry for
Lightning in naughty lingerie.
My tongue is knotted fishnets

On a decapitated head.
Its brain plopped on sawed-off legs
Never thought of again.

A HUGE SWARM OF HUMANS AT RISK OF STARVATION

On the bathroom floor, they pass out
And stink to satisfy nature's need.

A rabbit's skull.
A raccoon's ear.
Mosquitoes from centuries ago in readymade snow.

Huge swarms of humans at risk of starvation
All look the same.

DREAM OF EVIL

Tons of cars are smashing turkeys but
Houses are built for us anyway.
My cause and the wind are old news farmed from cold throat meat.

Your breasts slice open your belly.
You're beautiful.
You're not coming back.

Old boxed pasta grows into a patient fly on my leg
Waiting for its brain to leave
The house I sit alone and burn in.

AS I DIE I WOULD LIKE TO HOLD

An unknown flower
I can attach a dildo to.

Chewed Eyeball Clot

A carpet of slug eyes
Breaks our bed
Some dishes are drying
I need to charge my phone

So there's death
To watch later

Share
Copy link
Tap to unmute
Any death I like

Maybe I'll wear my new sexy underwear
To the swamp tomorrow
And click to share
Vines cut away for the exit sign

Sometimes I wish my woman
Lived with another man

Sometimes my woman
Wishes she was dead

I get up to meet the day
But see I'm not around

The things that hold me up
Are getting old on the road now

An abandoned head
A terrible age
An inhuman time

Holes in the frozen pond
Sipping blood clot soup

Oceans reach outrageous flood levels
Drinking blood is easier than smiling

Like my dead grandmother
I spend more and smile less

But without making a purchase
I shoot the cashier in the head

We were more friends than lovers
We never needed to touch each other

I wake up early
To hunch over my desk
And smell my neighbor cooking a dog

A perfect indoor light writes
The child in me is dead
And my dreams are gone

I'm a wall that plays with sex dolls
I'm a bird that shits out walls

I'm God riding
Rolled-up fast food bags
Lost to themselves

In this perfect indoor plight
Waking up early
To hold it wrong

The cases are rising
And her hands feel wonderful
But I'm trying to get out of a family

I'm a man of
Releases and changes
Causing souls to fail

Black holes and plastic wrap
Answer me when I'm striving
To end

By willing a hand
Taking off my skin
To throw away the sky

When I'm looking for nothing
A single father drives into his garage

The garage eats him alive
And I'm inspired by bathing in his overflowing blood

What was once known
Is what I just thought

The future's bloody and underserved
The future's bloody and deserved

A me
Hops on delicious piss

I live my life
Something left of nowhere

Frogs between my eyes and nostrils
Get me by

I put my faith in
What was once known then lost

A sunburn on the snow
Cooks our baby
Caught out of nowhere and
Watching TV from a playpen
Not sure what variant it's carrying

The hemorrhoids in my nose
Are surprised by the spring snow
My eyebrows leak floods
Of black bug blood

We all come and go
Blind faith in the Earth is our deepest thought

I wish I could laugh
About my heart always breaking
But it's different now that I'm poor and aging

My favorite tree
Tries too hard

To be a cold winter rain
Hovering over a cold creek's shame

A hungry owl
Barks like an old dog

My meat in its beak
The world has changed

My baby's eyes
Into cricket songs

My face looks the same
As it did before
My

Grief and buffering
Going back outside
To survey the backyard snow

A warbler shows me love
As I roll my son's ashes and smoke them
For an origin of the ceiling

The wind is picking up
Blood fond of bagged
Moss animals with their robes undone

I'm going back inside
Smelling like an inhuman time
Growing into life

A dark tree
Pisses in the snow

The snow's piss
Makes delicious mist

I'm on my drugs
Staying all night in my blood

Something flies by
Melted ice burning flowers down

A single mother pulls into a garage
Her groceries sprout hooves

I am inspired by waking up
Her wrong blood

I say goodbye to the dirt on the snow
As you get the drinks

It's beautiful to be afraid

There's nothing more important
Than taking off your dress

For a wolf's chin returned from the night

Looking at some snow-covered spring daffodils
I'm moving inward

Into that long black cloud
That black
That long cloud

The long black
That

Thickening fog on a dog's throat
With a face battling mine

The trees smell like
An arm falling out of a suitcase

The blackbird dances
Then gets laid
He works hard for what he craves

I throw an apple core to the satisfied fucker
And he tells me I won't figure out
The meaning of my life

As the graffitied ass
Of a to-go box
Standing too long in the same condition

The blackbird got laid
But that's over now
His mind is a deep red cloud

Stubble I missed with a dull razor
Stabs at shrunken chicken nuggets
Dropped into a waterfall
Drowned by another waterfall
Memory means too much to me

A worm trapped by the robin's stab
Plays dead to welcome
A place that's never been seen
But grows bored in a belly
Because there is no conflict

Wood ducks perched on a local billboard
Advertise the latest chicken sandwich

A facemask on the model with a sanitizer rash
Eats the latest chicken sandwich

The traffic light glued to her forehead
That's where I'm going

My reward is smelling her new panties
Without end

She plucks a gray hair
Before blowing me

Her mouth is large
Her gray is natural
I am dark to myself

Shredded garbage bags for miles
Tire after tire over tired worms

Walnuts hide
The skunk hit by a new car

A baby bird
Tears up and chirps from the street drain

Cages replace benches
In a park that one of two suns slaughter

What I was
I want now

I couldn't help
But fall in love
With all kinds of rain
From all kinds of times

Dull creamy or brownish
Sexual worms break free from
Pierced plant stems
With old brains trying to forget themselves

Life grows into a rain
Trying to forgive itself
And I've ended up
Like a bony ant with nothing but

Feeling the wind
Roll it up into a ball
Being kicked around
Until a heartbeat is felt again

A green heron
Rides a water snake

It's okay
We're all insane

This polluted canal
Layered with muskrat dumps

Is what I love
It's what I trust

The thing I'll always be
Is scheduled to finish charging

Apples and water
Breathing and beer

I've made a prison out of
Discovering no more words

I've made a prison
Out of a lifetime I'll never live again

I make a pond with my bloody knees
And kneel in it to play
A sandwich containing a fish

That cheap breakfast thing
Everyone haunts
Is ready

Don't buy another book
Be bored with life instead

You never know when
Half a tree will piss on half a dog
And unsayable towel racks
Move real slow

I killed an ant because it bit me twice
That's the closest thing we've ever felt
To a family

I'm walking in the heat
Because I like to feel sad

A horsefly rubbing her legs together
Has all value

I don't know
A crow with no bones

Walking in the heat
Because no one knows the name of what's to follow

A salamander grows
In the leaves under my beer can

The salamander knows
The dirt at the bottom of my soul

Every bush and stone
Is a dead leaf full-grown

Beer cans are my soul
Missing the innocence it's known

Octopus bird noses
Drown together in a sludgy puddle

After not listening
To plastic bins singing

About what's missed
When sad girls dance

To nothing more important
Than to know God's not listening

To God feeling
The icepick up a rainbow's ass

I love every moment
I invent my own doom with

I lock the windows
To keep the frogs in the creek out
Then they really start looking
At what can get them

Like a bowl of fake lemons
Waiting forever in a cheap tree
Underneath parking spot debris
Feeding on me

Two skies of crooked moths
Sewn into my clothes
Believe in
Summer breezes during a plague

I find you without my phone
We're in love again

I stick your phone in my mouth
And we wait

Until half a sandwich abandoned on a bus stop bench
Discovers it has more words

You stay over
And then I leave

To become a dead ant
On a faraway boat ride
To where the world strikes
Its final empty pose

I'm searching for a parking spot
And blow a gnat out of my nose

There's no power in my apartment
So I think more about my life

Each morning there's chains in the sky
And waiting deer

Each morning there's days
Weeks and hours

I'm looking for a parking spot
After being away

Every day I've lived is in my head

There are doors shut

I'm finally inside
And you beat me to bed

You beat me in bed
Digging up history

Appliances and devices
And a million things that think

A million things to think about
Doing all over again

Play toes
Play toys

I don't know when
I'll never do anything again

I'm learning how to die
Like three cars parked with their lights on all night

I take a good look inside my mind
And have its dream again

A plop of bird shit
Lands on an old man attached to a rolling walker

With his hunchbacked wife behind him
Carrying an oxygen tank

They saw excess skin on their arms while walking home from church
They feel everything that isn't there

They stop at a bench in front of a public library
To kiss plops of bird shit

Dark wings of a drone fry the sky
Boiled refrigerators yearn to cry

Loose tobacco in the boiling water

A popping flea on the screen door

I'm tired

Come fuck me

I go out for one more smoke

Because I'm afraid of my big hard cock

And wanting to do nothing with it

I've changed

You've changed

A rainy frog is oiling

The trap door

We sleep side by side

Automatic Hallways

MYSELF

Tears of plagues.
Eyelashes of teeth.

Blinding life.
Absence of life.

RATS WILL RUN UP YOUR LEGS

Life is man boobs
Decorating bundles of shot kids
Grinning like shattered school windows.

Their smothered phones
Discover menus of each

Distant mountain
Reading taint
Beautifully.

THE WIND IS GETTING WORSE

And its eyes growing tired
Slice open every
Bathing rat ball.

A witch made from toast
Eating feathers with wine,
Casts life catching up with me this time.

The creek is hungry for trees.
It just sits for a while and balks like
Who cares

That I care about the lonesome whistle of a leaf,
Eggs beaten by a vine,
A warm fish hanging from the color of the sky.

LIGHT AND SHADOW

Her gushing cum show
Of indifferent wax stenches

Laughs at the way my ass stinks
When beetles eat dried tadpoles.

CLIMAX STAGE

I don’t dream.
I don’t scream.
Beneath my ribs are rat-pigs
With children’s arms.
I foresee my death
And am too tired for it.
Bats hang in a hiccup.
Such is life
Reorganizing my yawns.

AFFORDABLE HOUSING FOR RENT

I spit in the creek.
I miss your pussy.

A carefree last sunlight,
I pretend it's not happening.

I spit on your pussy,
But you don't like that.

I am bored with water.
Let me make your pussy wetter.

Let's watch tits and ass
Get a handjob.

Or listen closely for the missing teeth of a bird call
Not remembering its last handjob.

There's pounds of raw chicken saving drowning
children
In the very back of my mind.

I love you
And don't ask why.

HOT AND NOT

I'm afraid of being hungry
In a public building,

With an odor of hot
Pancakes of insects

Dressing a pregnant child
Free of wonder,

Huddled in a plastic building
Headed into the not.

IN FRONT OF A SHRINE

My limbs are parched.
Hair is my flesh.

I see omens of skin burning.
I seek no victory.

I've abandoned my life,
If I was ever there at all.

I beg for meals smeared with star shit
On mac n' cheese bones

Inside the striped snakes
On the flooded street,

From their floating cracks
Black ants

And virtual flowers
Leap from an exploded airplane's bathroom.

There was never enough time
To use my heart.

GODDAMN EVERYTHING

A popular robotic vacuum
Has sensors that map and remember my fingers.

It never smells,
And every night before I go to sleep

It's knocking on the walls,
It's chewing gum in my brain.

Its bones are lifting right out of its vacuum,
And flying through closed windows.

And my body separates like a puzzle
Of chattering teeth and hairy jaws.

I buy more stuff
To knock pieces of my veins back together.

What I order
Puts my head where my feet should be.

My arms where my ears should be
Are automatic hallways

Gunning down everyone who uses a bathroom.
Goddamn everything.

I WORRY ABOUT ROADKILL

When she kisses me passionately
We remove our tongues.

We're dancing behind the backs of
Broken asshole news.

The stars are discarded water bottles
Amazing

Meat that walks up a hill
With eyes of short rainbows.

COUNTLESS BLACKS

I love machines
That tell me what to do,

That tell me I'm tired,
That tell me there's nothing around,

But baby ferns and blind worms
Living for the decay of my mind.

Mice in ice
Panicked with a doll's disease.

Dwarf wheezes.
A bird sting.

Something I have
Stuffed together.

Something I gave
Stupid and colored.

Behaving like anything
Supplied between emotion and spasm.

I love being arrived,
There's everywhere left to die.

PUBLIC SEX

Permits me to be a monster
With slugs hammering out my teeth,
And an ability to buy and take
Nausea by the dry pond.

Rising anus,
Crystalized monument to
Shadows of piss flowing down dentures
Praying to the Christ forwarding a chicken wing.

I am your dirt on a damaged doll.
A sheep with cramps.
The blind jawbone's menstrual blood.

Death's direct eyes blow
Lots of packaging longer than life
Cloning skin under the sleeping penis
Of a daughter's chunk

Paralyzing the rock
Seen by a sun
Nothing understands.

DISTANCE FROM LOVED ONES

Drowning in carnivorous insects,
I visit the decay of every animal alive.

The common toad's
Poisonous cottonmouth

Shelter of porno mags
Flowering bloodthirsty

Mud turtle tentacle rainfall
With no hind legs inside its shell

Wading in shallow water that looks like lobsters
Not caring about themselves anymore.

WITHDRAWN FROM THE WORLD

A floating leaf in its climax stage
Pulls down my pants for dying people.

The clits on one guy's body
Touch noses in acts of recognition.

Dog food's shiny wet coffin
Glows a thousand colors of lovers

Planning on anal
As painful as a sacred fire

Delivering the dying universe from evil's
Simpler minutes.

WE PUT AWAY OUR SEX TOYS

The sterile throbbing
Of a sour ankle's summer

Had a brief marriage
To the smell of the floor.

A way of life
Of nothing more.

The holy ghosts of lettuce products
Being recalled

Fly away astride pickled blades of mud
Afraid of any female with eggs.

Only a damned fool
Would write anything down.

Muskrat, hooded merganser.
What does the light around their bodies matter.

ALONE BEHIND THE HOUSE

I'm thinking about sleeping and too much sorrow.
I'm plastic wrap blasting through black holes to find a
  family.

A napkin hearing itself being crumpled,
My eyebrows squirt floods

Rolling over swarms of cages
Glued to turtle blood smacking the spare parts of trees.

Sleeping just isn't happening.
Crunchy wasps burst

The sexual stages of mall beef
Living for free.

SLAIN TOT

A murderer across the street
Chases his recyclables from the wind.

He's paid for a genetically modified wife
Cooked into the ceiling.

Their joy is washing dishes
In a jumbo roll afterlife.

It gets me down
That I've traveled so far and this is all I've found.

My dreams are mostly a drag,
Just another cheap way to understand religious music

Bugs enjoy when they slurp salads
Wiggling like green moons crashing into double
  masked desires.

NOBODY IS SAD

She comes home from work early
To show me her nice titties,
Then we eat avocados.

The upstairs neighbor packed in his wheelchair
Talks to shopping bags
Keeping him warm.

Shopping bags know who their real friends are.
Seeing nice titties helps remove my scars.

I come home from work early
And beg the clouds to stuff me.
Avocados in their wheelchairs shop for naked
  neighbors.

A closed gas station blooms
The dead in a video taking their blankets off.
Nobody was sad.

HOLINESS

Misery in society
Loves me like no other.

I'm with the woman I love
Watching people in their cars.

They look like freshly delivered boxes
Trafficking people inserting fogs.

I love living things
Escaping their lives to reframe the same

Burial in a tree of boxes
Breathing hot container breath.

Confusing food package labels
Stand quiet in the rain.

The woman I love
Is chopping off my cock because I don't mind

Being cooked dickless
So no food gets wasted.

If only I could fill my heart with
The reuse of contaminated land.

A PLASTIC SODA CONTAINER LID

Underneath these napkins
Made for people
Made from people
Born for nothing
But killing sprees killing

Zoo things on fire
Burning with
Assorted pizza slop
Swooping under cop cars
Touching their lips to mine.

Some rain
Enters its first container bid,
Changing the sex of a napkin
Into ashes
Kissing me like a tinfoil place.

LEGS WITH HEARTS

You once had an ass,
And a crack for your ass.
Little flowers
To watch the sky.

CLOUD STUDY

Chewed-up rainbows make me slow,
And more human
Discussing violence with a frog.

What's waiting for us
Beyond hungry reactions,
And average sunsets framing the fences.

We troll dead kids in my dying phone.
Drink shitty beer.
Let another year float by.

That cloud is a public park pond carp
Shitting out a spider's egg opening its eyes.
My heart is a game

Germs and pavement play
With dying families in a dead phone
For delight and entertainment never screwed by old age.

The frog splits apart
From drinking too much beer.
His sludgy spirit rises

And mimics a blessed cloud
Not coming back
Because tomorrow is trouble and tomorrow is pain.

LIFE IN A POND

A plastic bag on a bush
Of plastic bugs
Barks at a plastic bush
Crawling with plastic bags.

A few of these poems first appeared in *Acéphale and Autobiographical Philosophy in the 21st Century: Responses to the "Nietzsche event"* (Schism Press, 2021).

RC Miller is the author of *I Get Groceries, Mask With Sausage, Pussy Guerilla Face Banana Fuck Nut,* the art book *Demon Drawings* (all with Schism Press), and *Abstract Slavery* (Dostoyevsky Wannabe) co-written with Gary J. Shipley.

He lives in Western Massachusetts.

Comments & sexting are welcomed at rcmiller23@gmail.com.

Also available from **SCHISM²**

The Birth of Venus – Rauan Klassnik
Xenoerotics – David Roden
Black Vellum – Ansgar Allen
Tractatus – Róbert Gál
Subconscious Colossus – Carlos Lara
Slow Hot – Andy Choi
Snuff Memories – David Roden
An Ideal For Living – Eugene Thacker
The Autobiography of Leisure – Narco Pastel
The House of the Tree of Sores – Paul Cunningham
Left Hand – Paul Curran
Coma Crossing: Collected Poems – Roger Gilbert-Lecomte, translated by David Ball
A Slow Boiling Beach – Rauan Klassnik
Serial Kitsch – Gary J. Shipley
Sacer – Nicola Masciandaro
Amygdalatropolis – B. R. Yeager
All the Messiahs – Anonymous
Thank You, Steel China – Sean Kilpatrick
Crypt(o)spasm – Gary J. Shipley
O Gory Baby – Brad Liening
Squeal for Joy – David F. Hoenigman
Pussy Guerilla Face Banana Fuck Nut – RC Miller
Spooky Plan – Drew Kalbach
Vital Signs – Tyson Bley
Mask With Sausage – RC Miller
Death Salad – Brad Liening
Drive-Thru Zoo – Tyson Bley
Necrology – Gary J. Shipley & Kenji Siratori

Also available from **SCHISM NEURONICS**

Perma Neon O – Oli Johns
Ponds – Nick Borelli
SATANITE – Snatch Wylden
On the Great Duration of Life – David Capps
Disintegration F_ace – Dave Brennan

Ω – 1 Chronotopologic Workings – Andrew C. Wenaus
Voidheads – Chris Kelso
Batesian Prey of the American Southwest – Sasha Hawkins
Pool Party Trap Loop – Ben Segal
Mineral Planet – James Pate
Interrogating the Eye – M. Forajter
The Selected Poems of Charles Tomás –
translated by Carlos Lara and Tamas Panitz
Book of Losses – Joseph Turrent
KRV – Oli Johns
Sorcererer – Jace Brittain
Sonnet Cycle – Tom Will
Burton's Anatomy – Ansgar Allen
Fall Garment – Paul Cunningham
The Isotope of I – Connor Fisher
The Reading Room – Ansgar Allen
You Alive Home Yet? – Daniel Beauregard
The Reaches – Ansgar Allen
> Get Back to Work – Jim Redmond
Everjescence – Tyson Bley
Work is Hard Vore – Philip Sorenson
Vagabond – Joshua Martin
The –Tempered Mid·Riff – Brad Baumgartner
I Get Groceries – RC Miller
Lynx Perpetual Lynx – Colin Post
Wretch – Ansgar Allen
A Large Retailer – RC Miller
Spelunker – Mike Corrao
Gynophobia – Tyson Bley
Normal Service Will Resume Shortly – Tyson Bley
Cyclops – Tyson Bley
Demon Drawings – RC Miller
Dark Poems – Tyson Bley
Frankencop – Tyson Bley
Celestial Chimp – Tyson Bley

SCHISM^2

Printed in Great Britain
by Amazon

39669447R00061